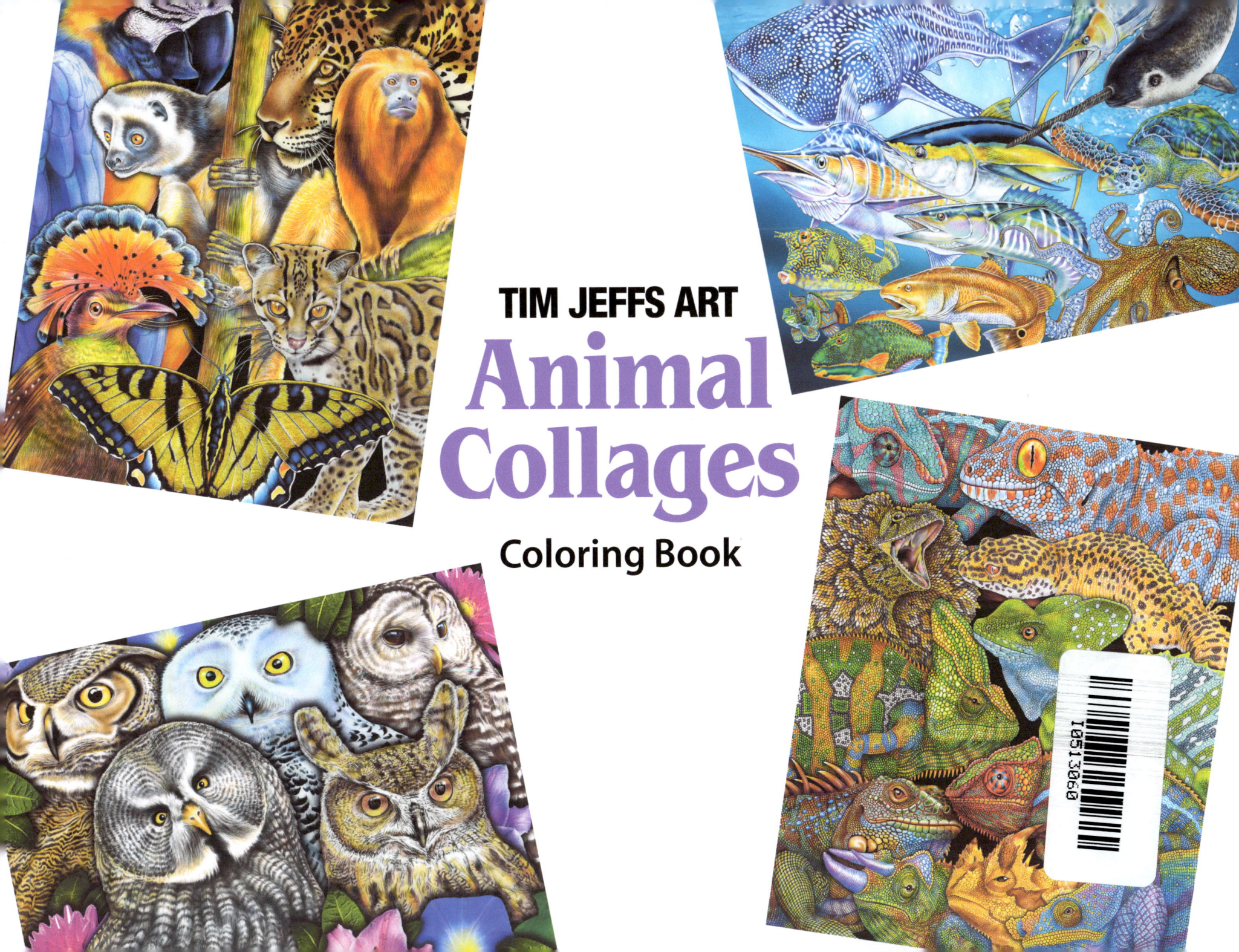

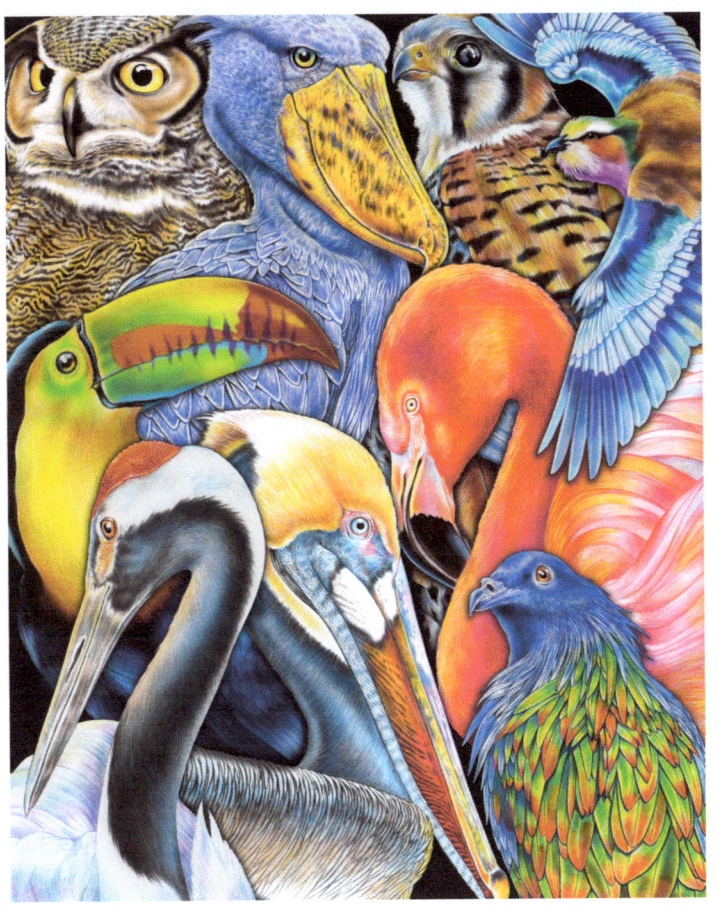

Building Collages

Just like a jigsaw puzzle. I'll never forget the very first animal collage I created. It was when I was in elementary school and my class was given an assignment to create a scene by cutting and pasting pictures out of magazines. I chose animals and enjoyed making it so much when I got home I did a drawing in the same way. I noticed when you create a collage in a way it's like working on a jigsaw puzzle. You can fit together different shapes and make a moving, living dynamic scene that takes the viewer on a journey around the piece of art. This coloring book consists of 20 animal collages I created from images I had drawn previously. By piecing together many of my animal drawings I am able to create themed collages that I hope you will enjoy coloring as much as I had building them.

Tim Jeffs
Wildlife Artist

For Jane, Jenna and Harrison
Dedicated to all of the wonderful colorists who have supported my art and made my drawings more beautiful with their colors, and all the precious creatures that we live among.
A special thank you to Jo Warren and Karl Jennings for all of their continued support.

© Copyright 2023 Tim Jeffs Art
All rights reserved. No part of this publication may be reproduced or distributed in any form without the prior written permission of Tim Jeffs Art.
Tim Jeffs Art
376 East Madison Avenue, Dumont, NJ 07628

Animal Collages Index

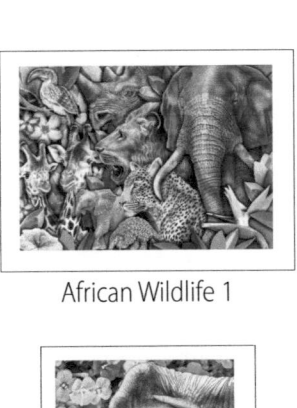
African Wildlife 1

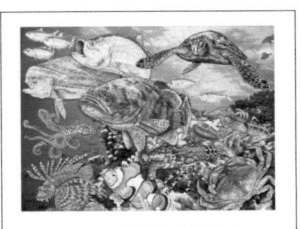
Coral Reef 5

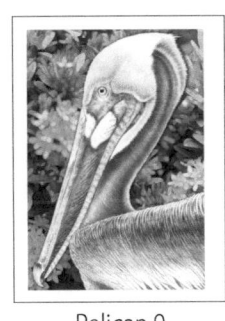
Pelican 9

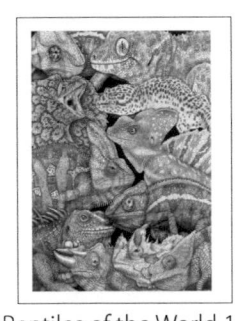
Reptiles of the World 13

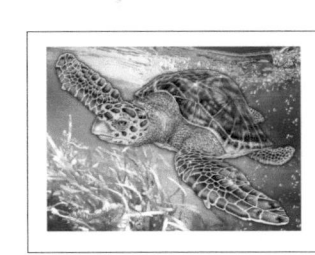
Sea Turtle 17

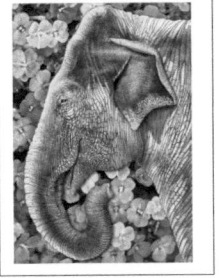
Asian Elephant 2

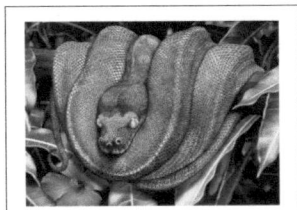
Green Tree Python 6

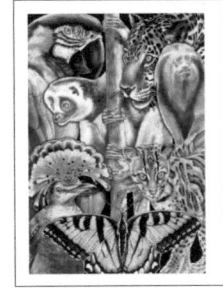
Rainforest Animals 10

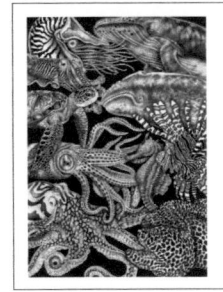
Sea Life One 14

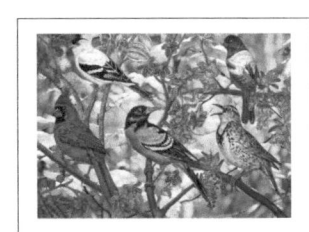
Songbirds 18

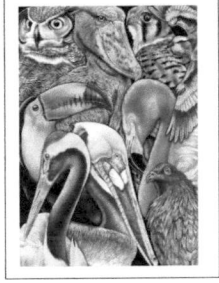
Birds of the World 3

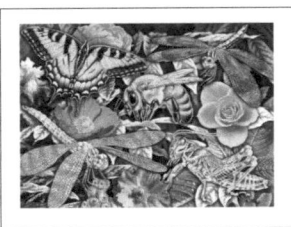
Insects 7

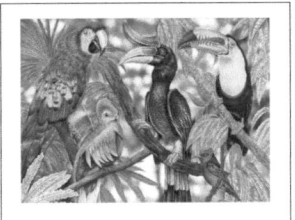
Rainforest Birds 11

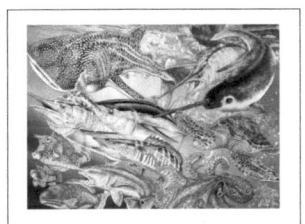
Sea Life Two 15

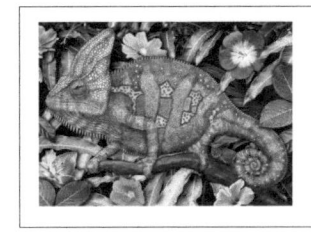
Veiled Chameleon 19

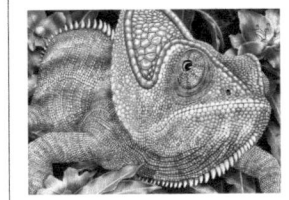
Chameleon 4

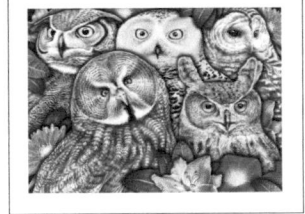
Owls 8

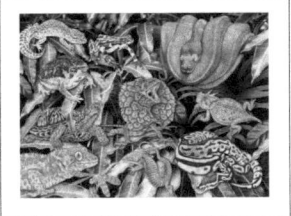
Reptiles & Amphibians 12

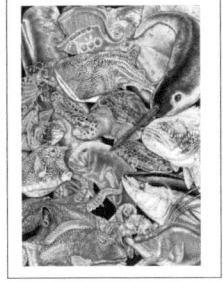
Sea Life Three 16

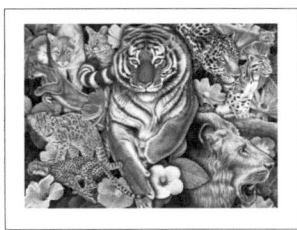
Wild Cats 20

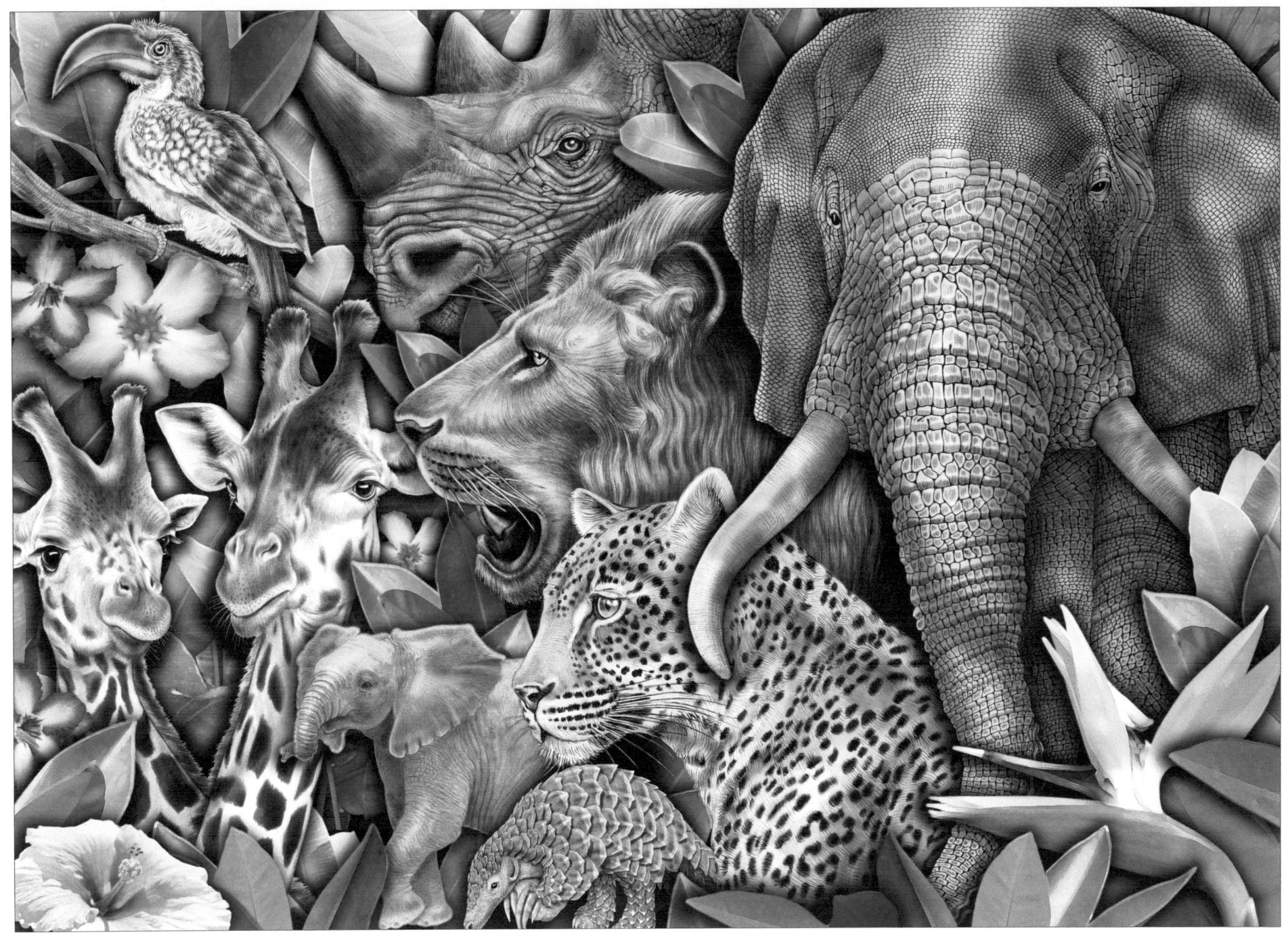

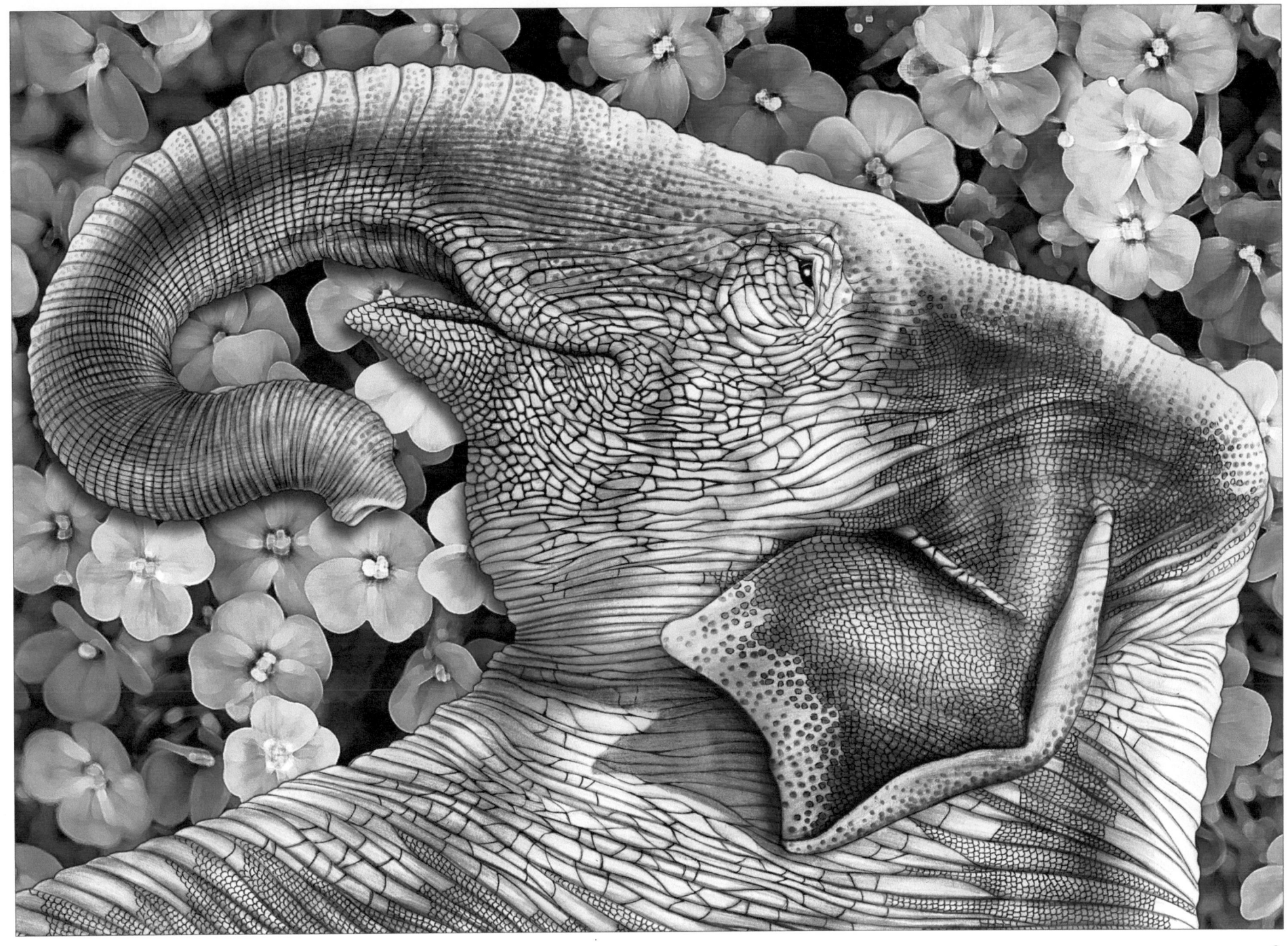

Asian Elephant

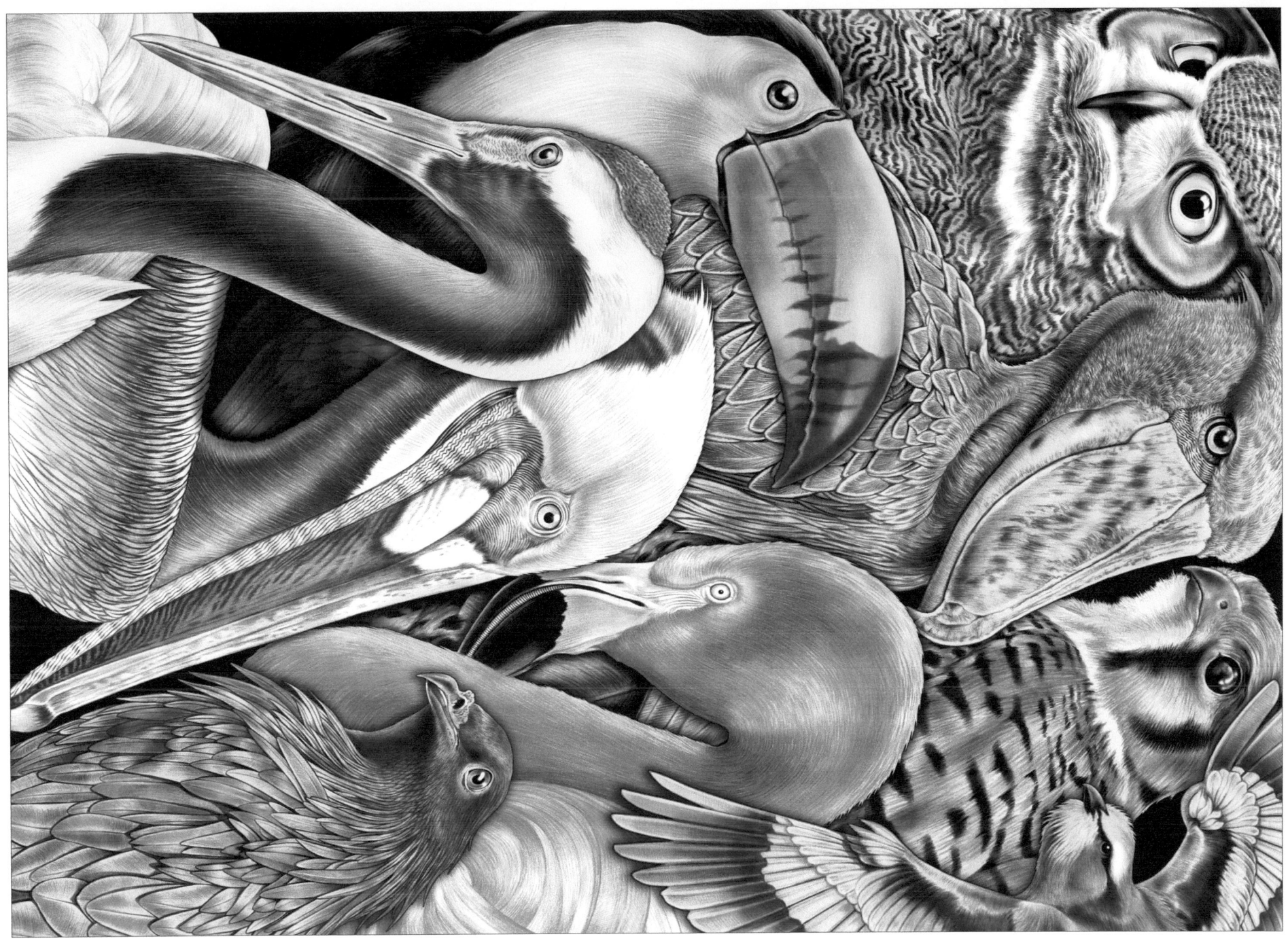

Birds of the World

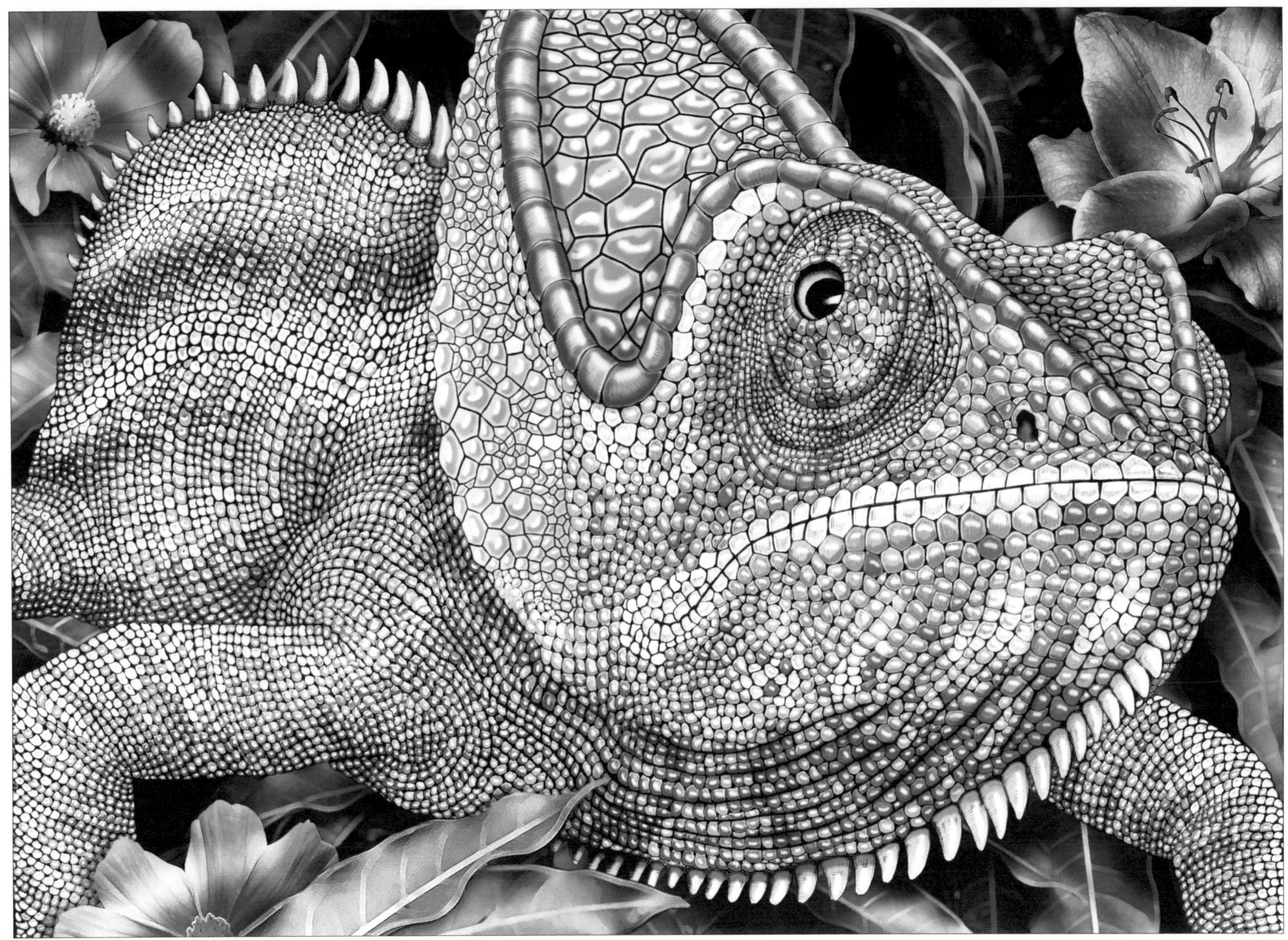

Chameleon

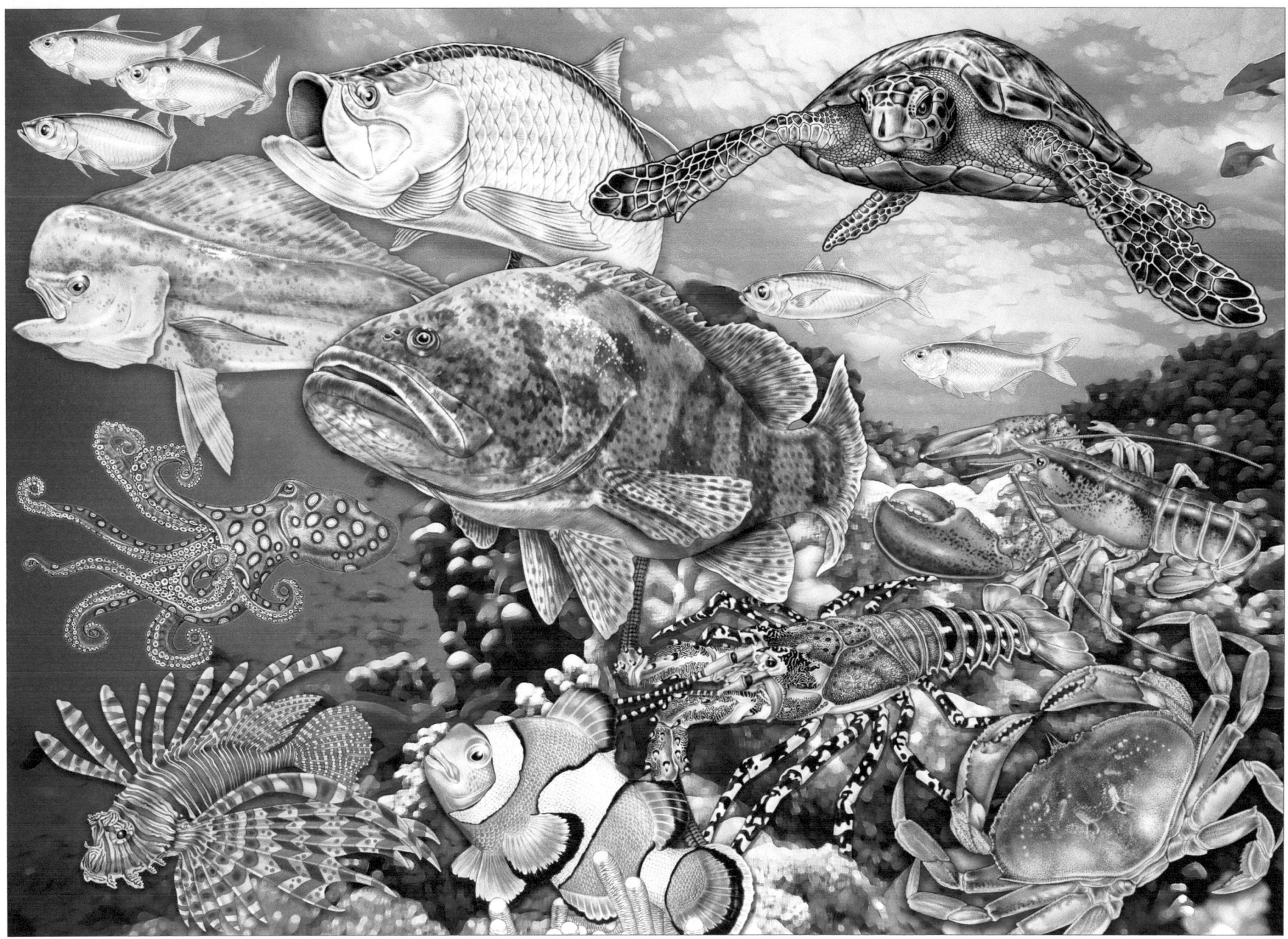

Coral Reef

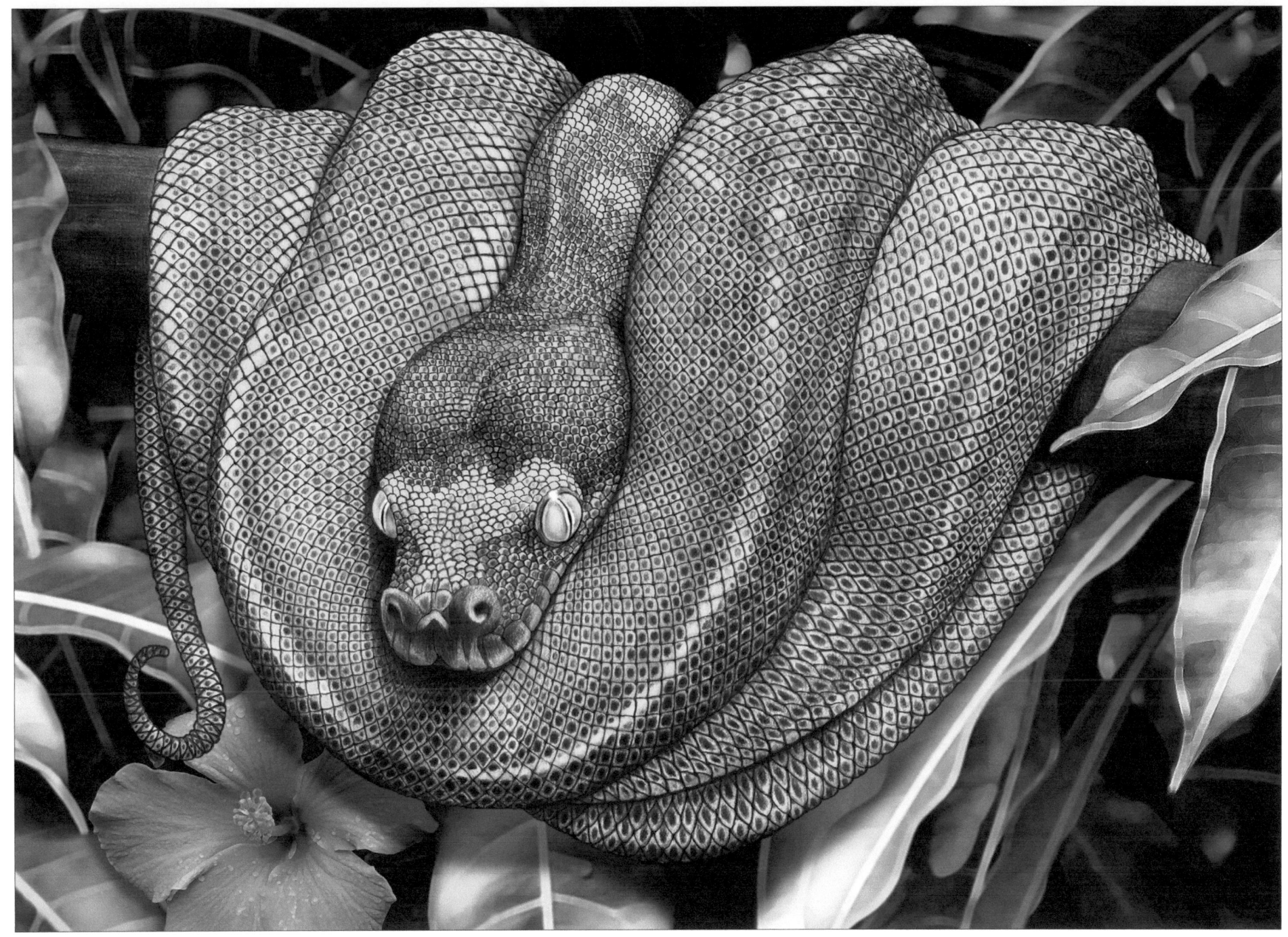

Green Tree Python

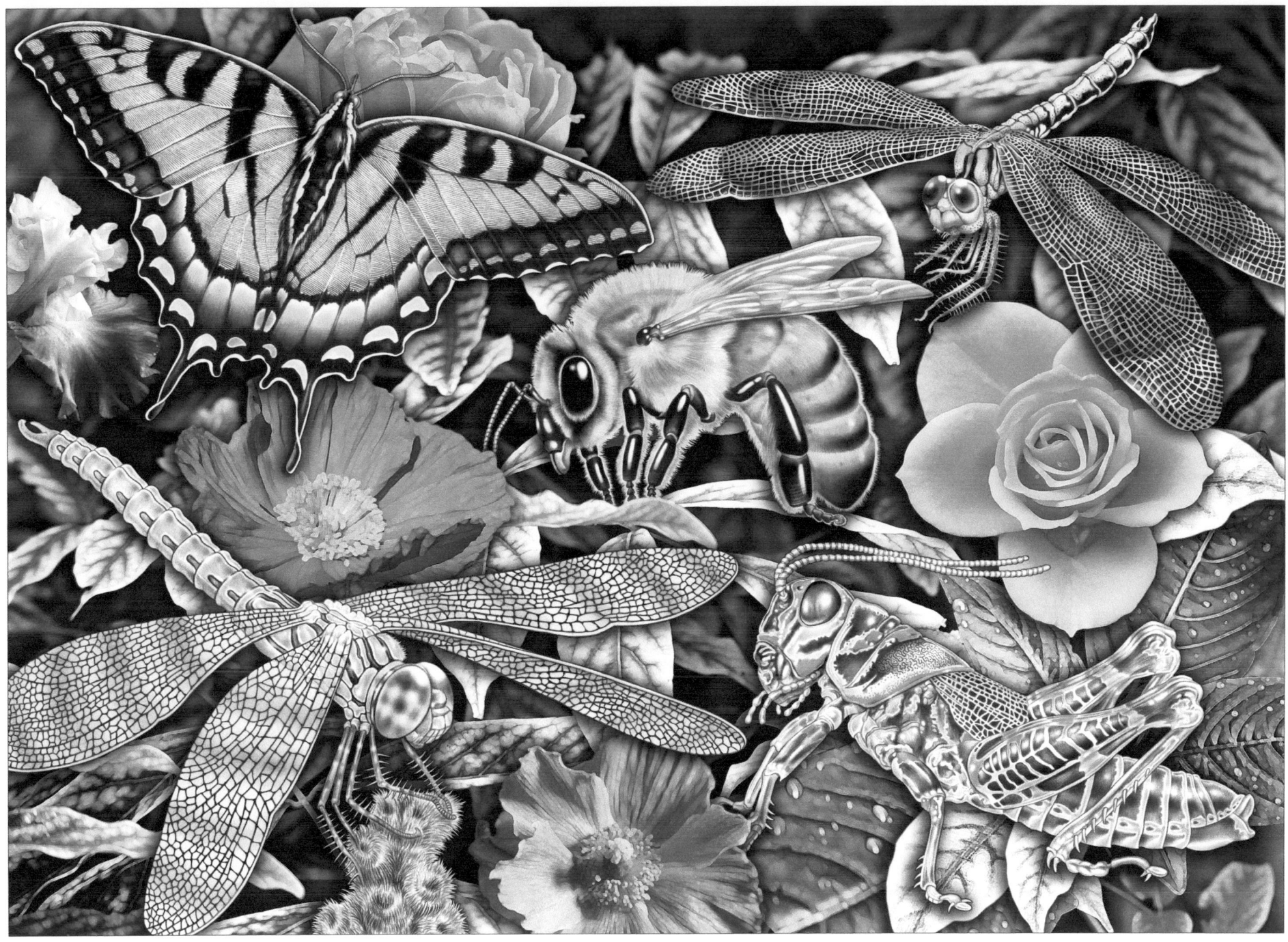

Insects

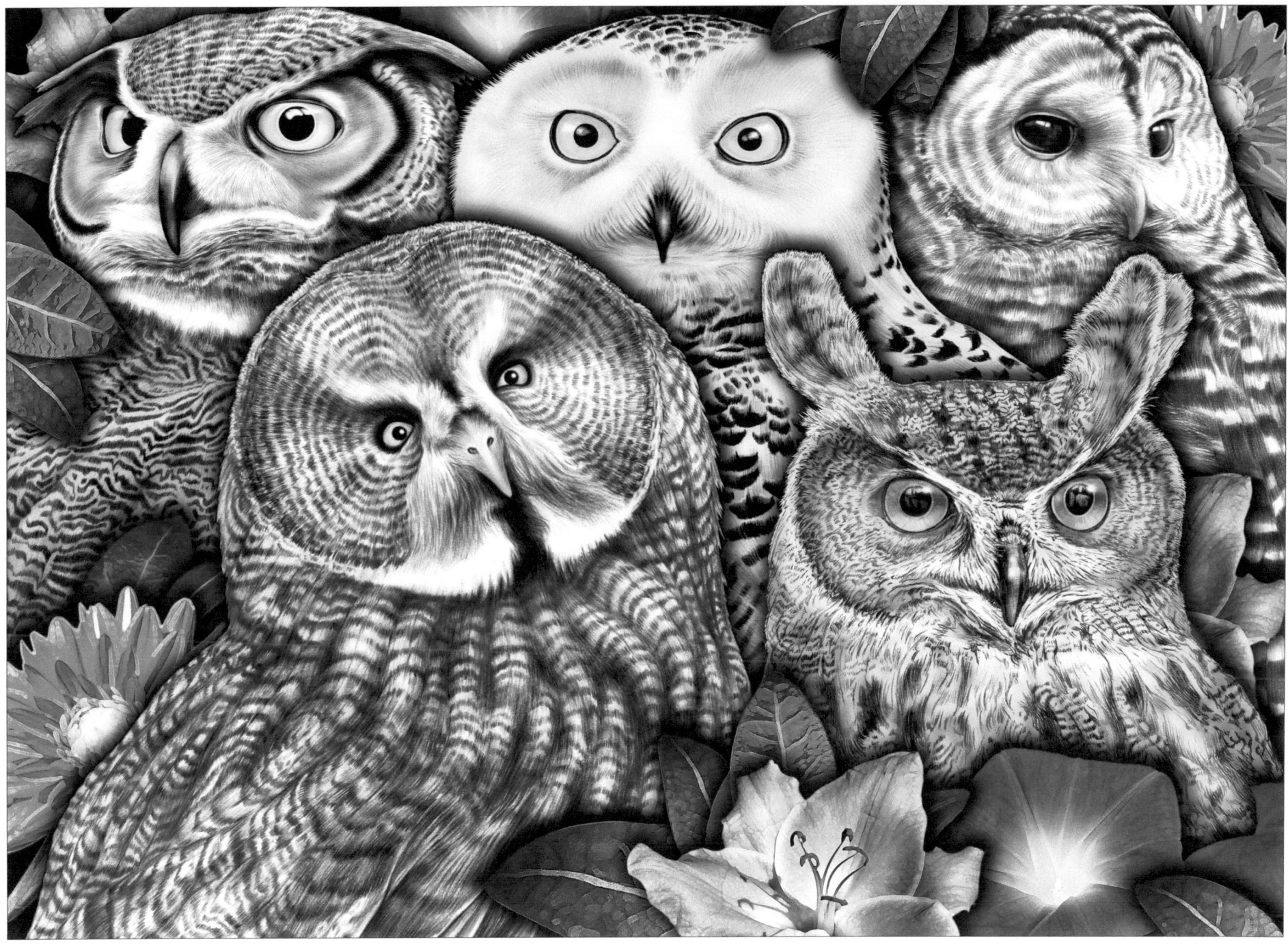

Owls

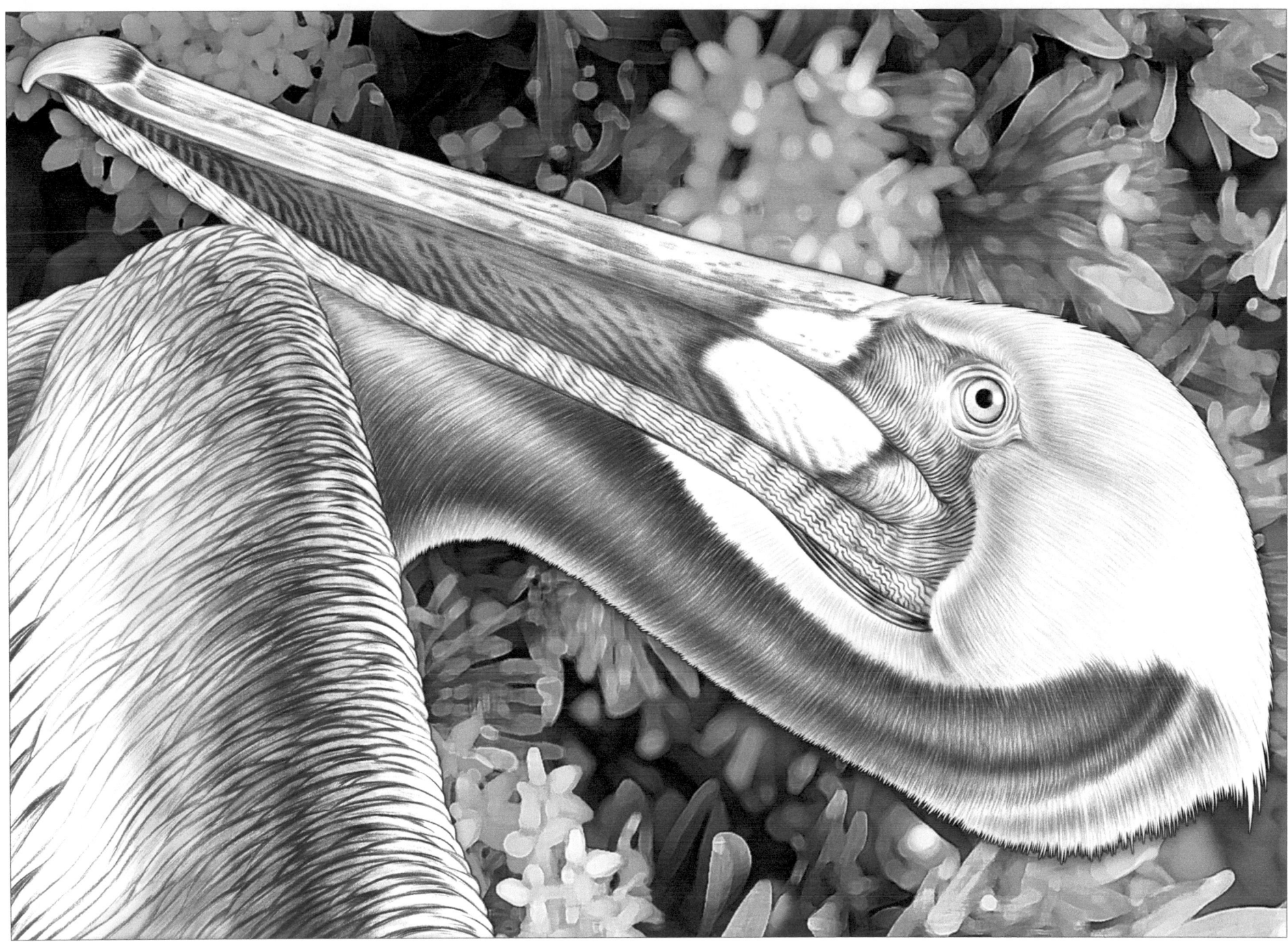
Pelican

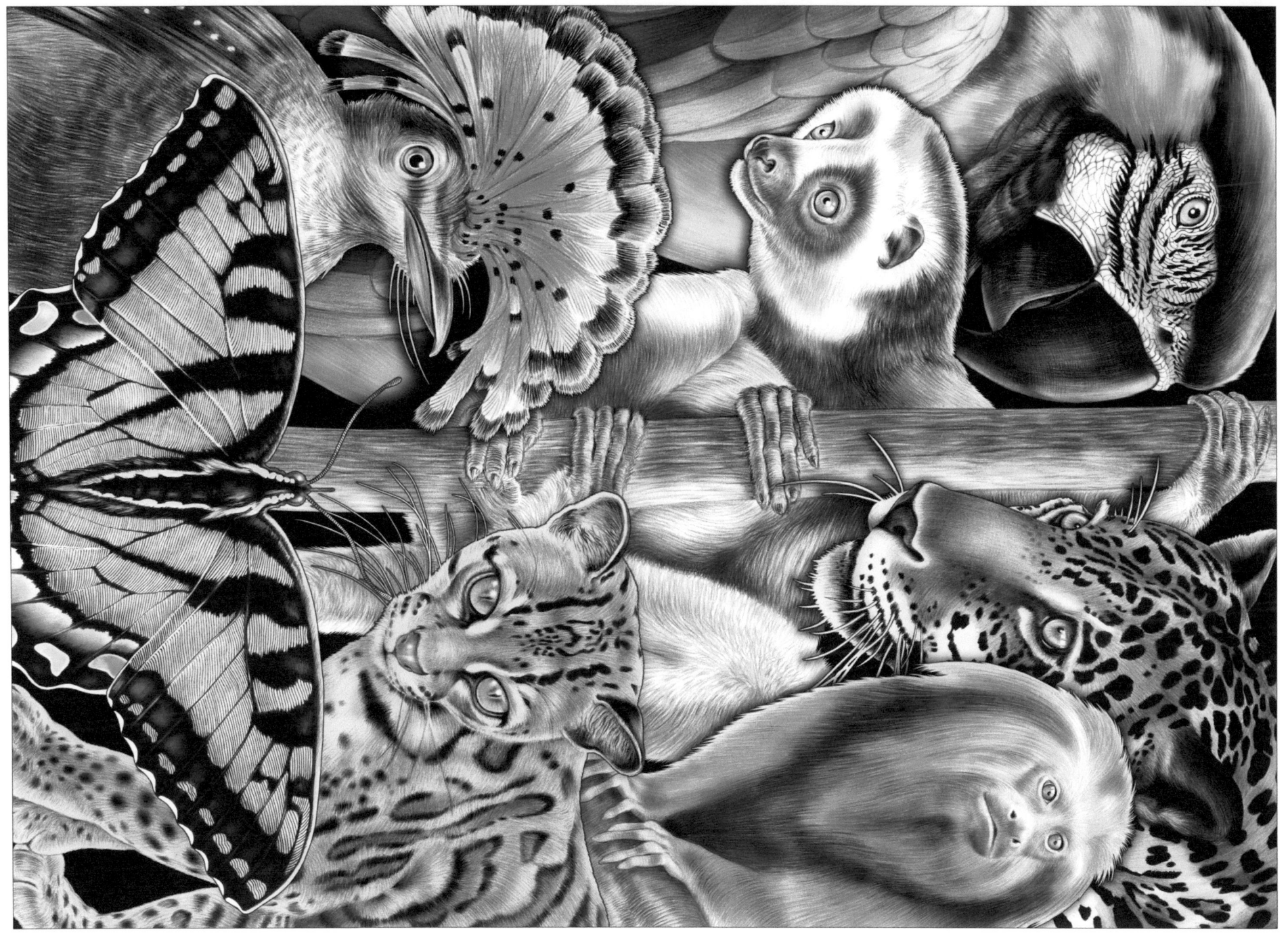

Rainforest Animals

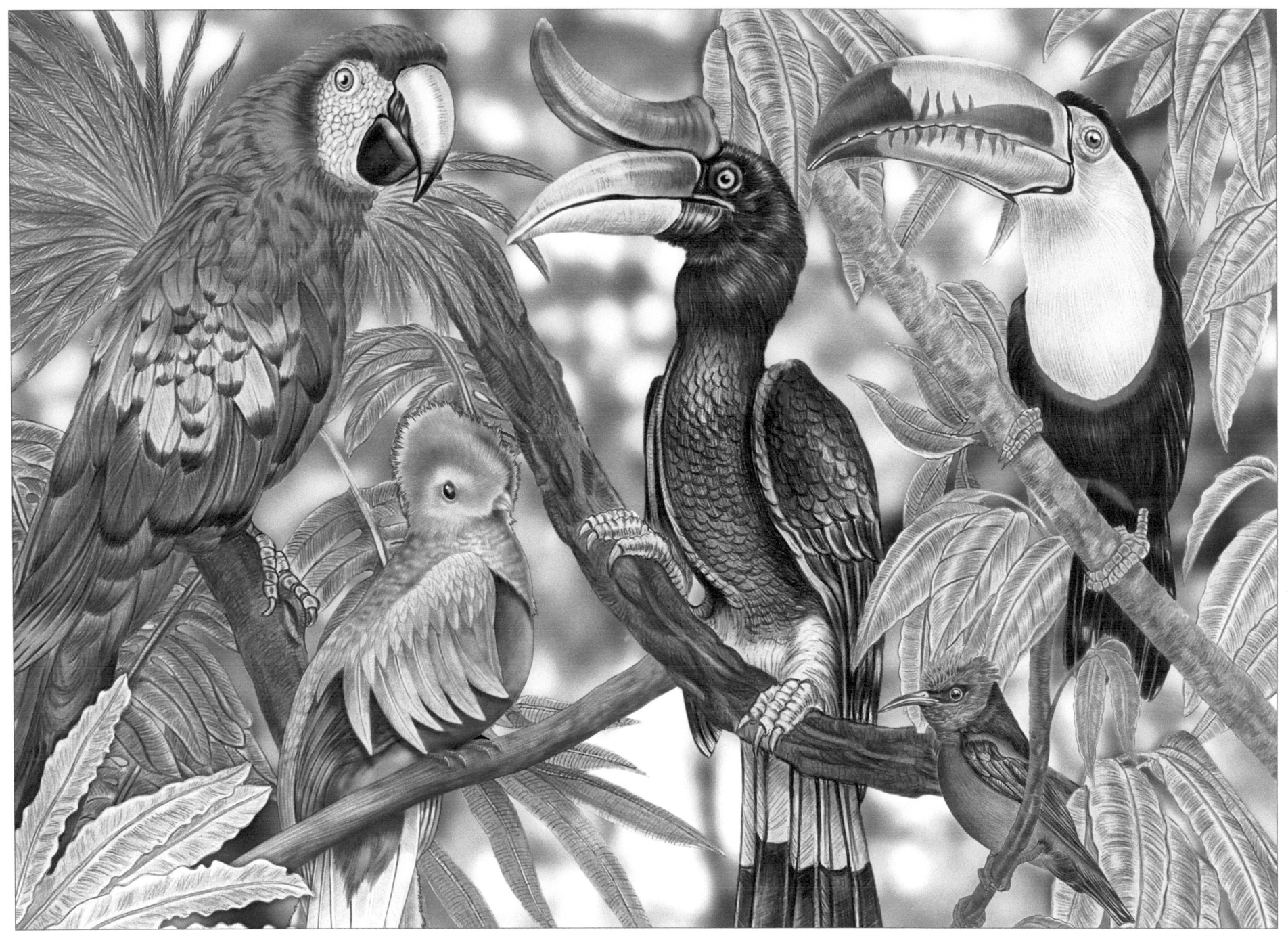

Rainforest Birds

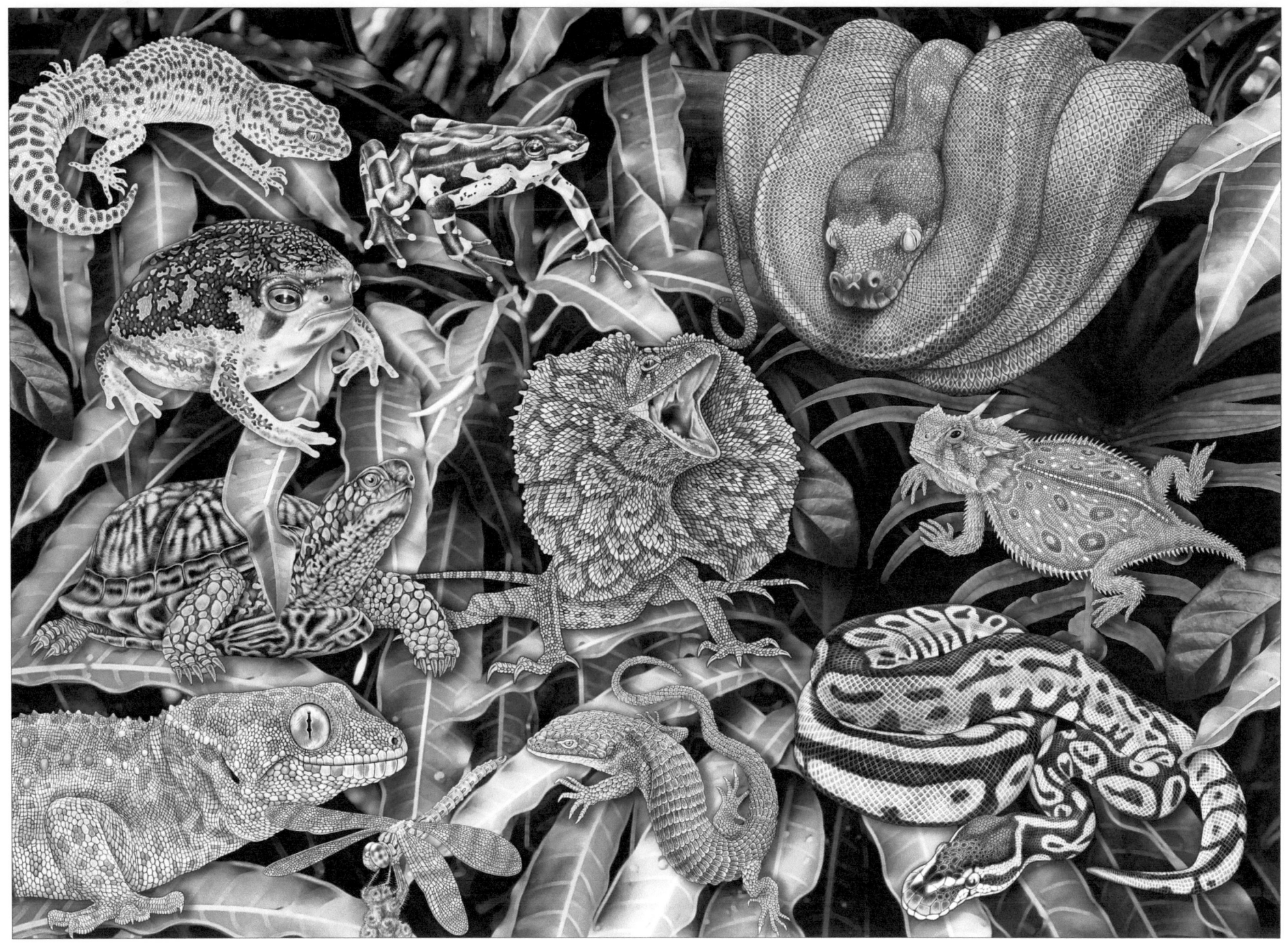

Reptiles & Amphibians

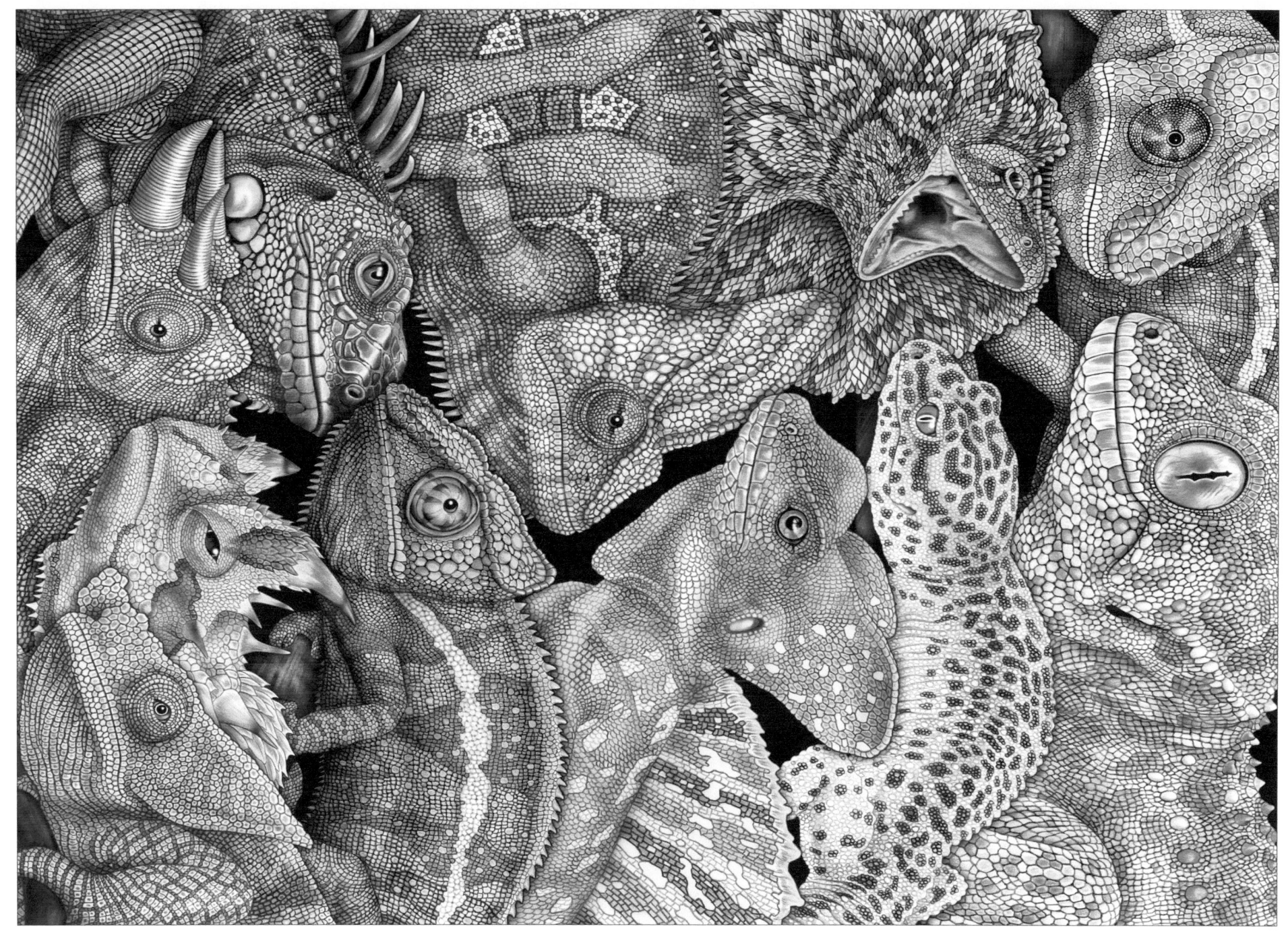

Reptiles of the World

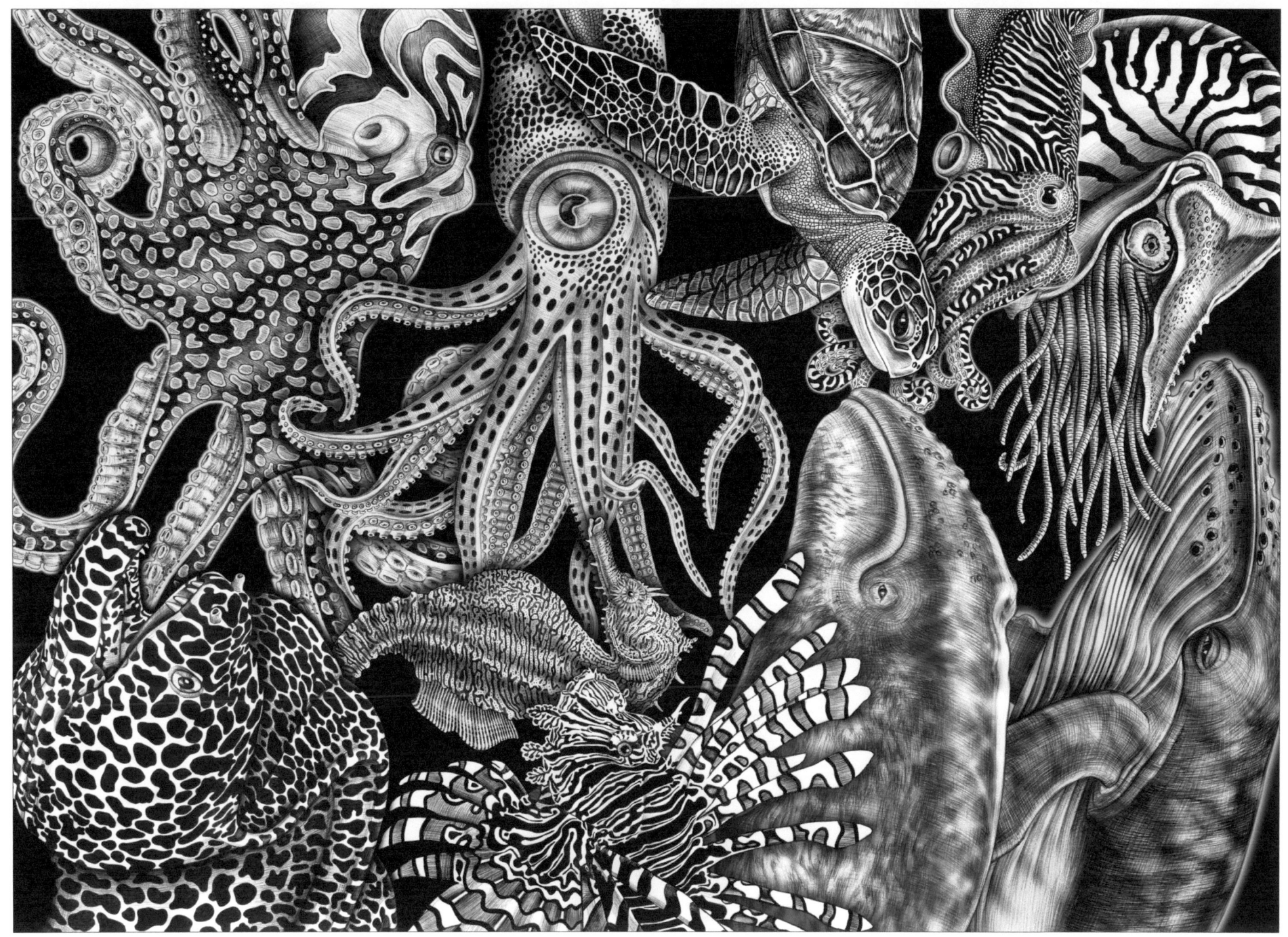

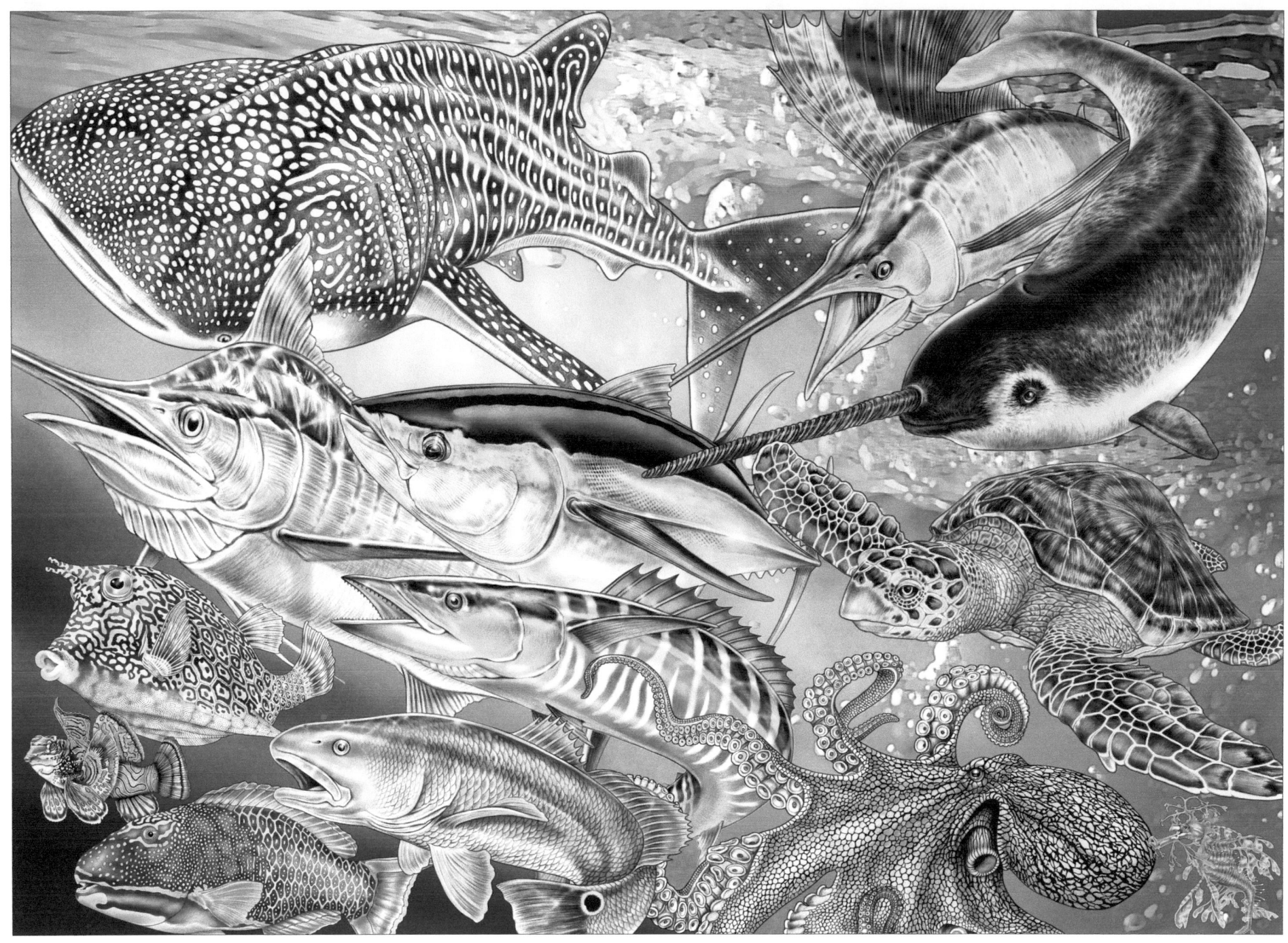

Sea Life Two

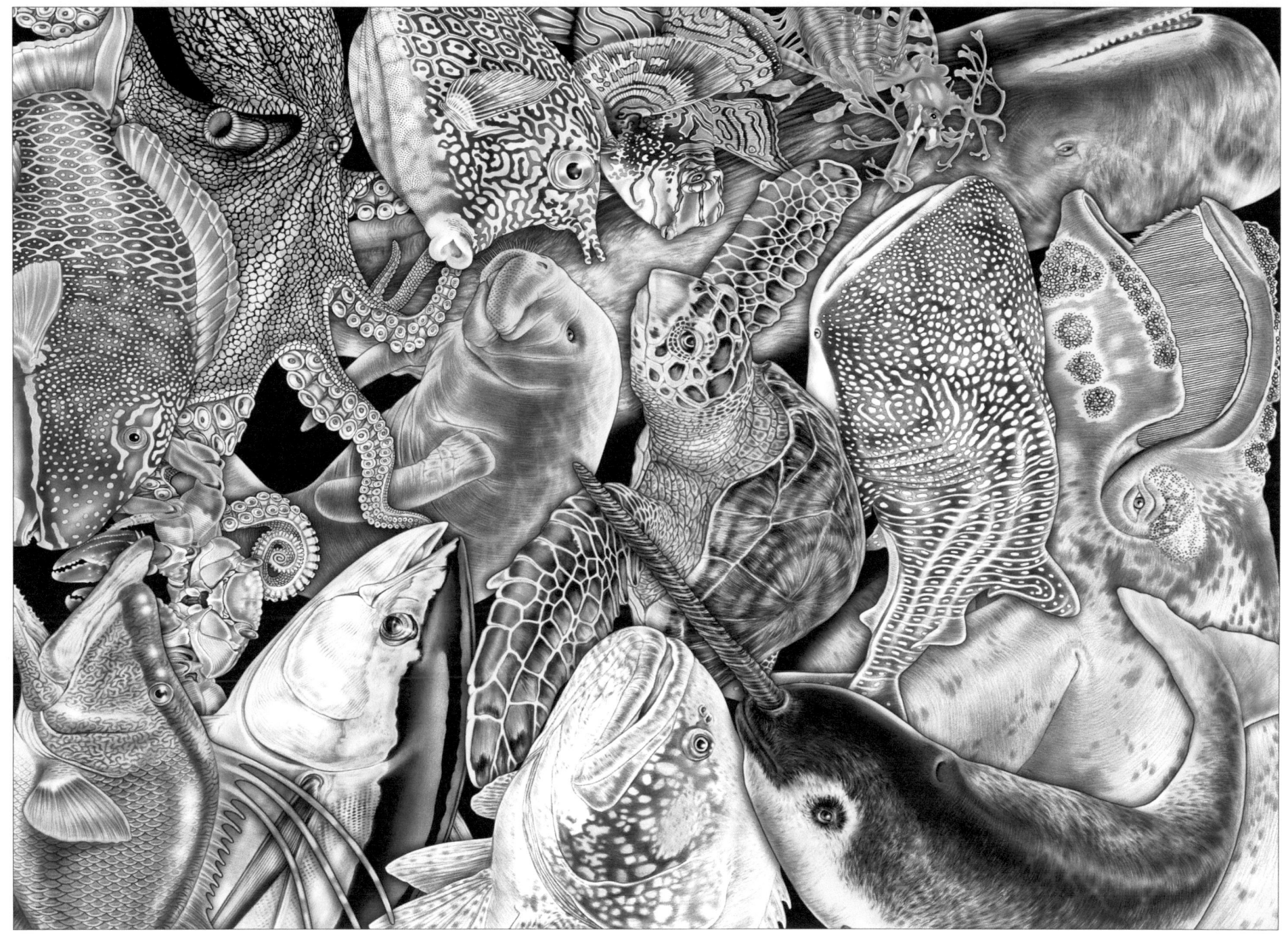

Sea Life Three

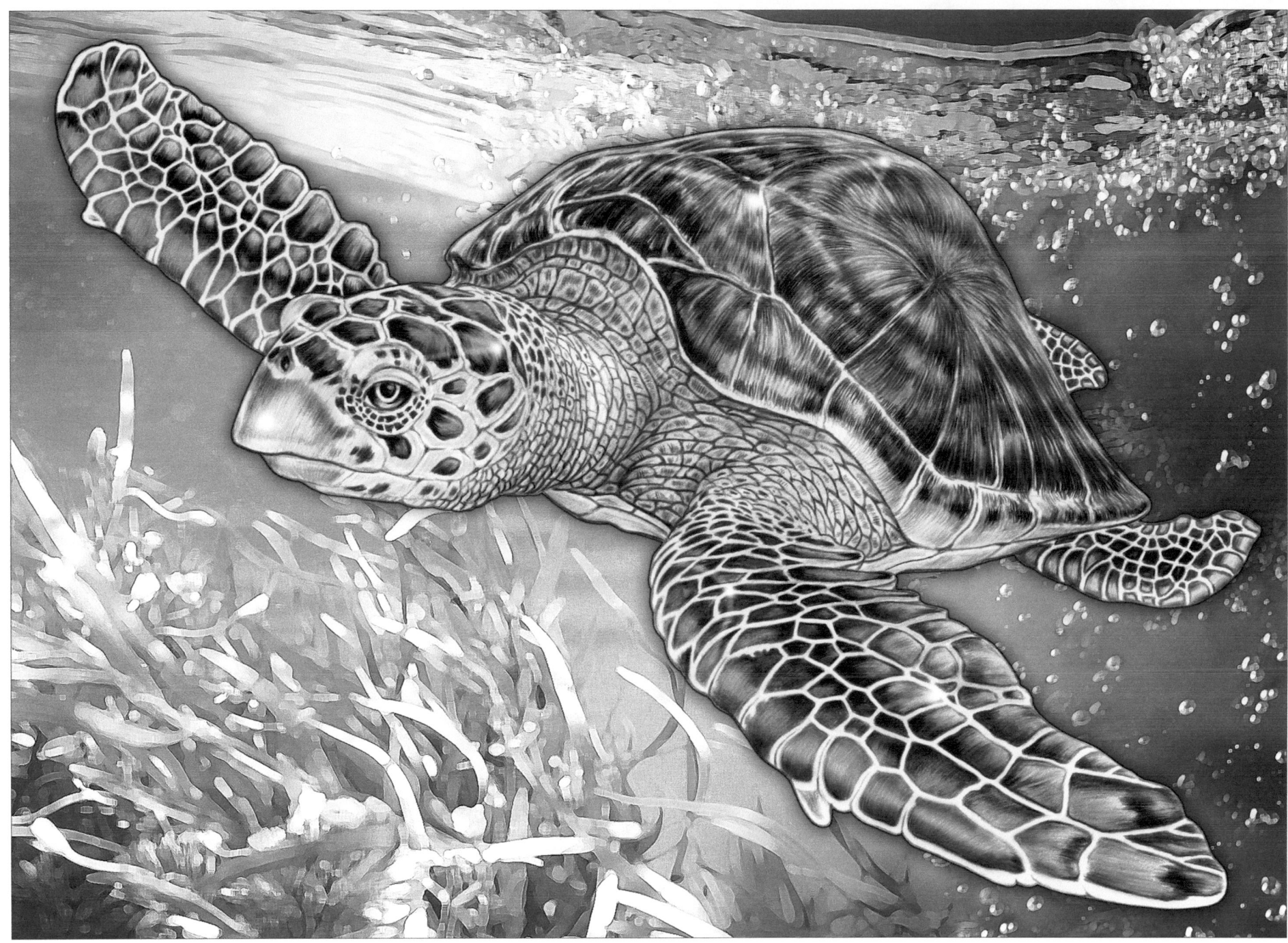
Sea Turtle

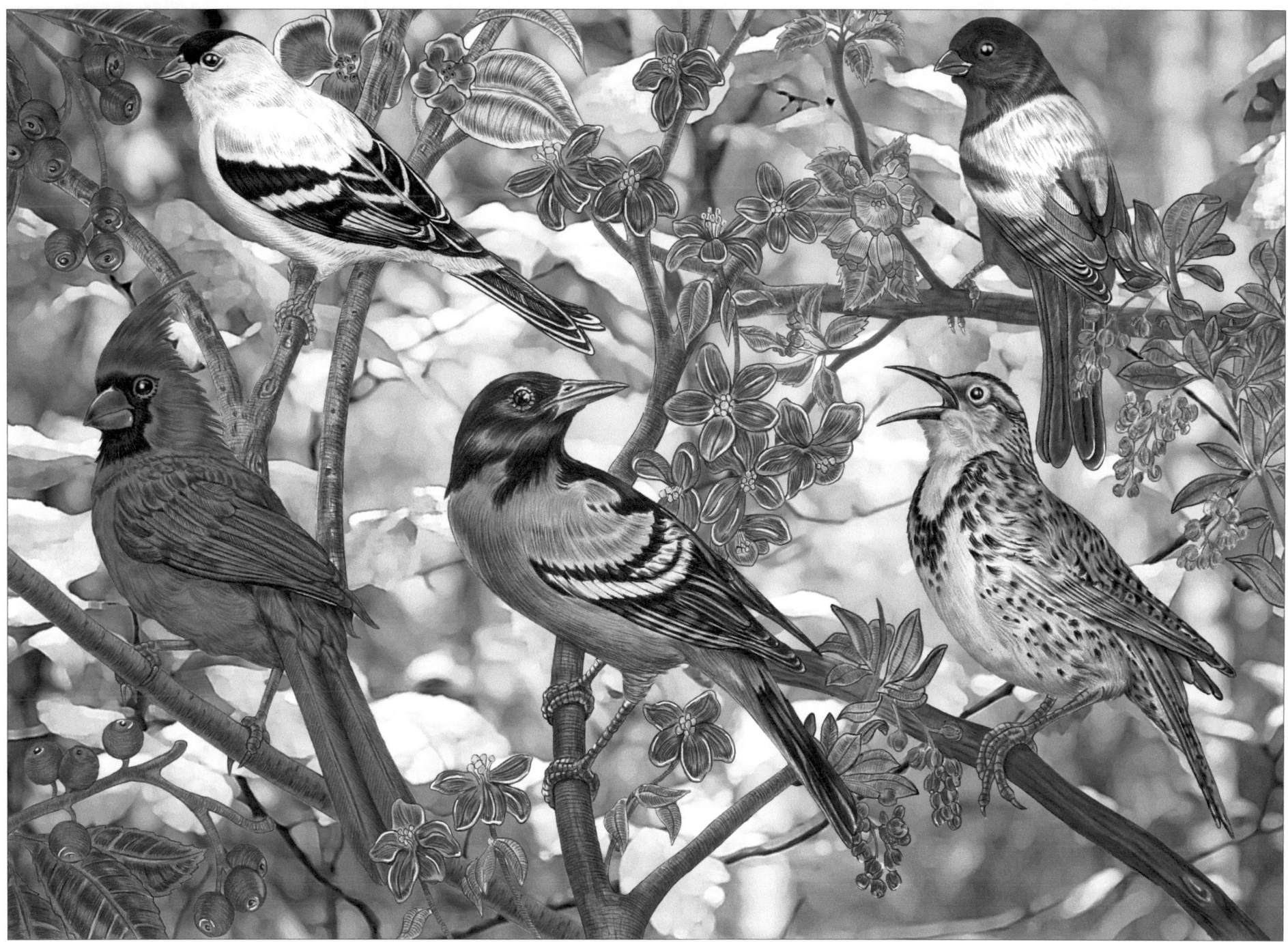
Songbirds

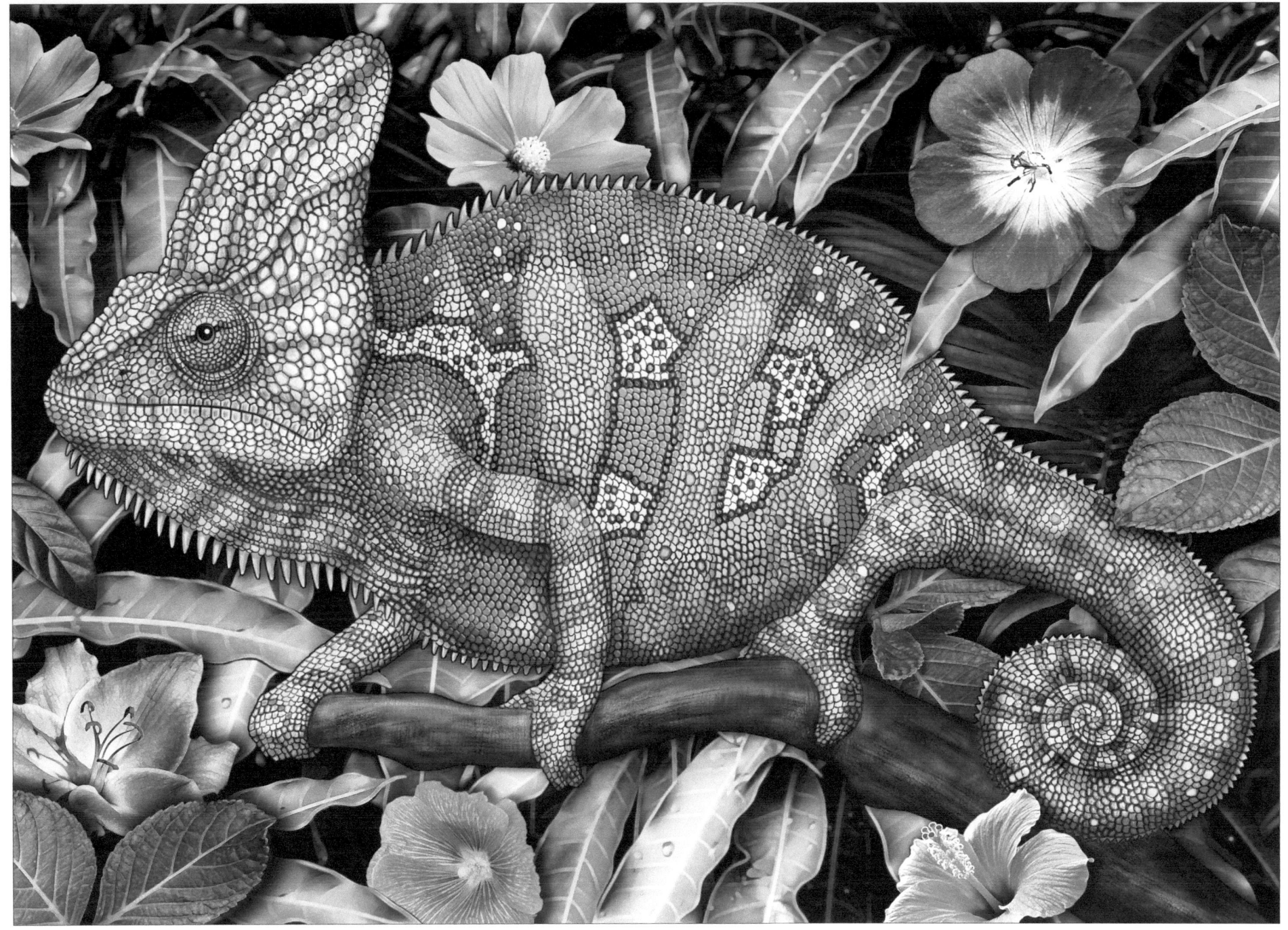
Veiled Chameleon

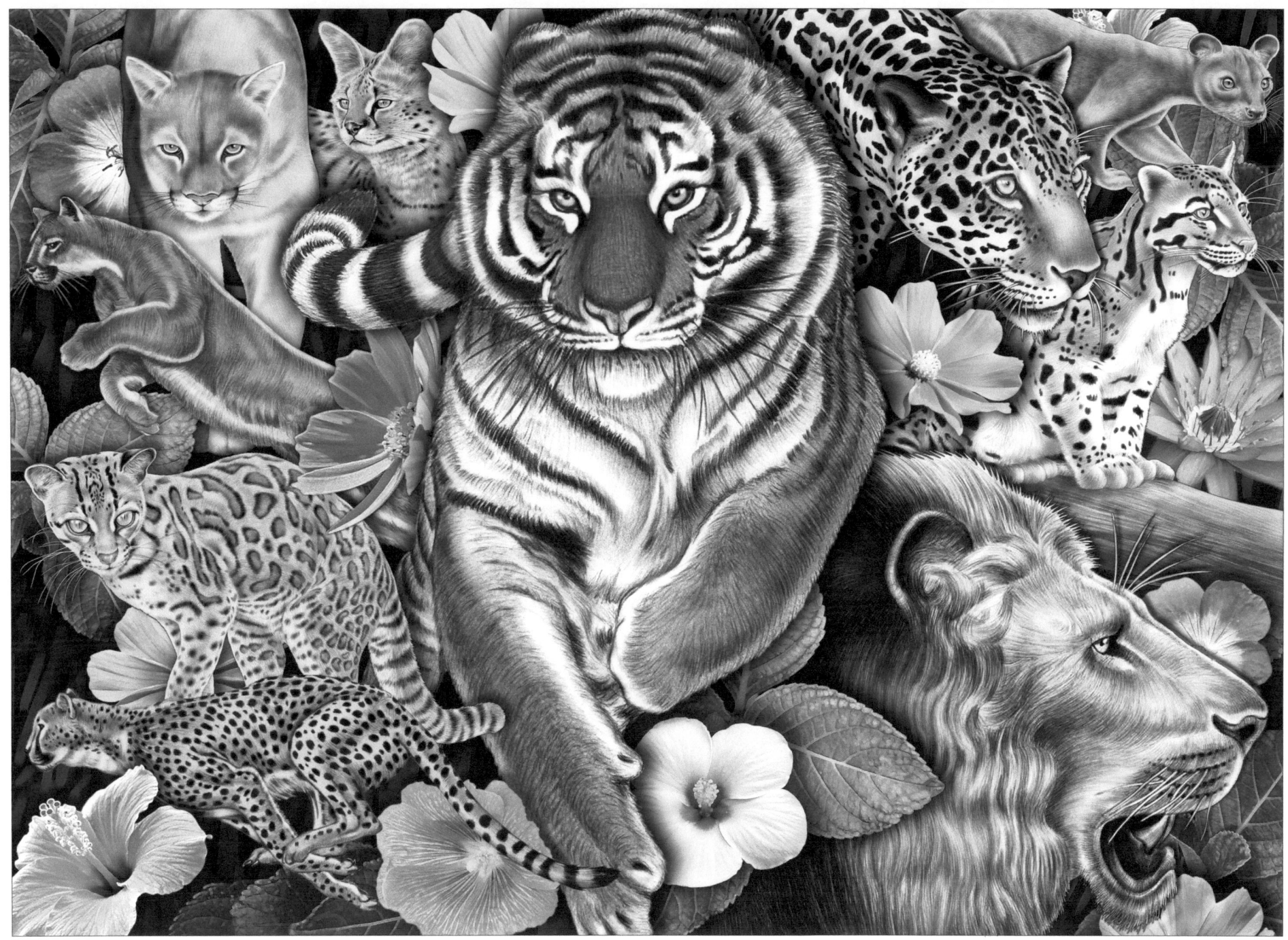

Wild Cats

Tim Jeffs is a New York City based artist and illustrator who has been creating dynamic artwork for over 25 years. Animals are a favorite subject matter of his, along with the complex and intricate details these creatures possess. "*The incredible diversity and complexity of animals has always intrigued me. They offer endless pleasure to look and marvel upon. In every drawing I try to capture the unique quality of each particular animal. I hope you enjoy my perspective, love and admiration of these incredible creatures.*"

Visit my website for prints, digital coloring books and coloring lessons:
www.TimJeffsArt.com

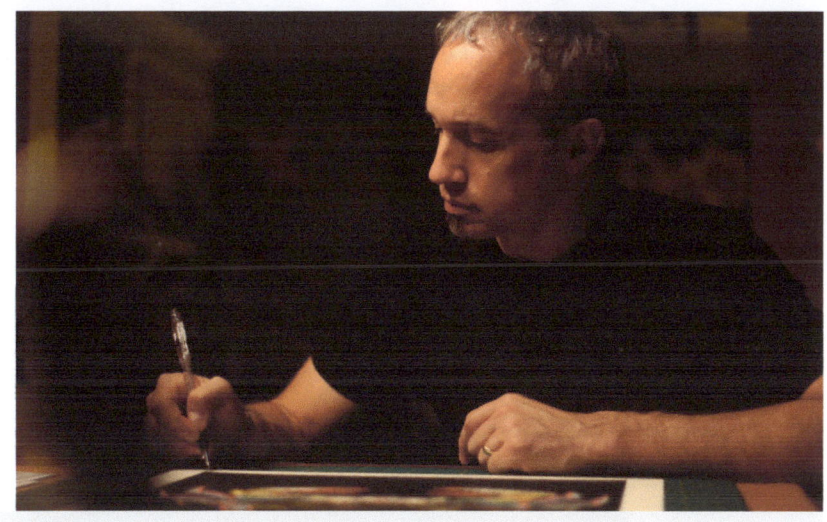

Discover the full line of Tim Jeffs' Published Coloring Books

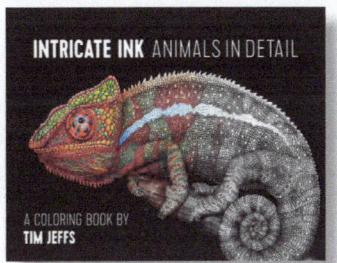
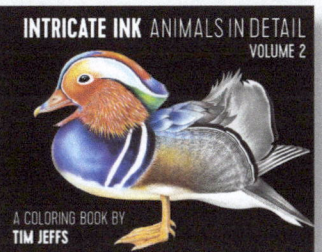
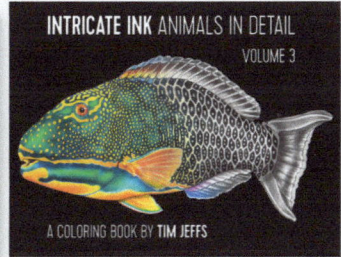
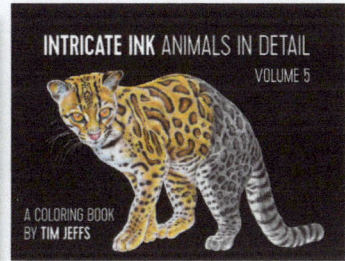
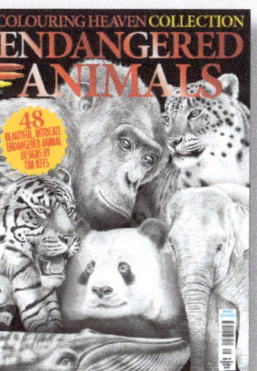

Intricate Ink Animals In Detail Volume 1, 2 3 and 5, and Intricate Animal Drawings Volume 1 and 2 are available at:
Amazon.com
Bookdepository.com

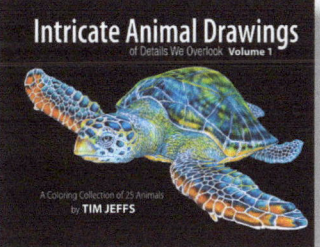
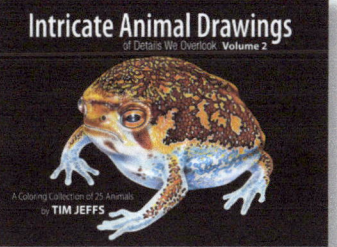

Colouring Heaven Collection Endangered Animals
Available at: Colouringheaven.com

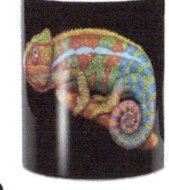

Discover Tim Jeffs' Merchandise

Etsy Shop
www.etsy.com/shop/TimJeffsArt

Society6 Shop
www.society6.com/TimJeffsArt

Redbubble Shop
TimJeffsArt.redbubble.com

TeePublic Shop
https://www.teepublic.com/user/tim-jeffs-art

Discover the full line of Tim Jeffs Coloring Books and Lessons at:

TimJeffsArt.com
Etsy.com • Amazon.com

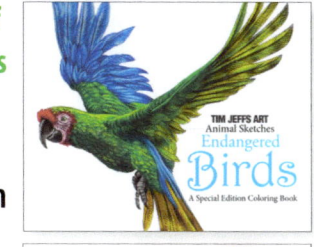 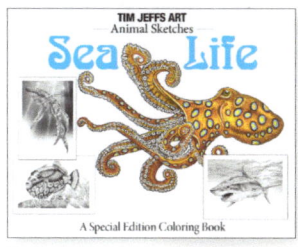 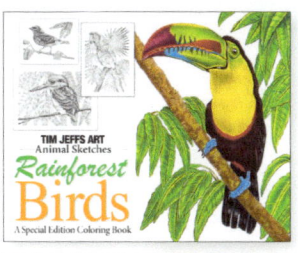 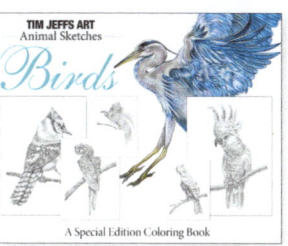 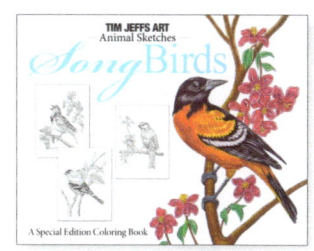
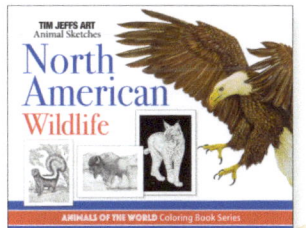 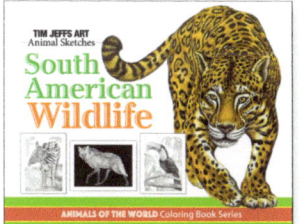 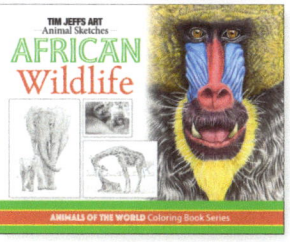 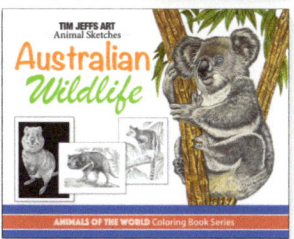 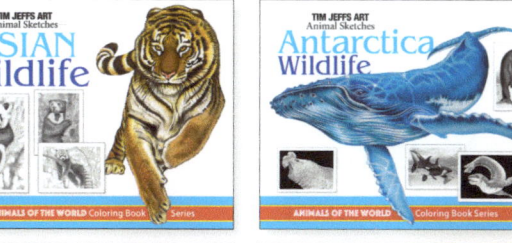
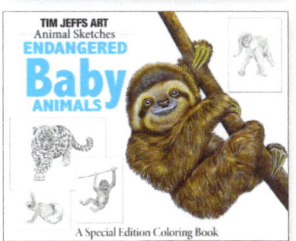 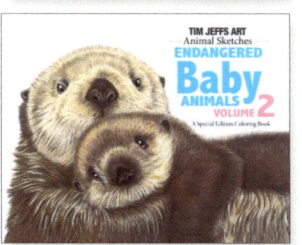 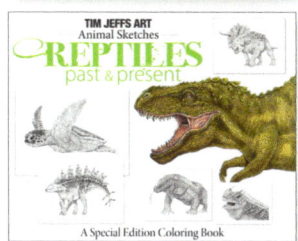 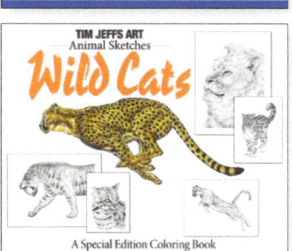 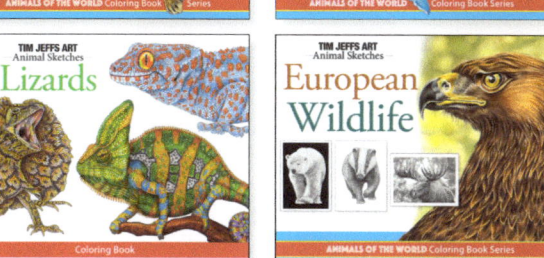
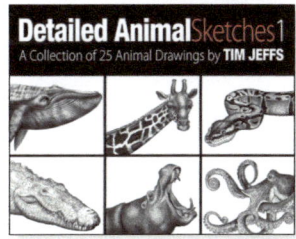 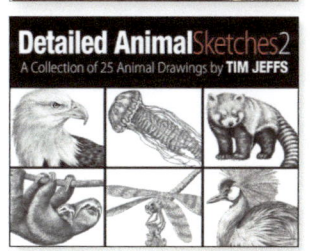 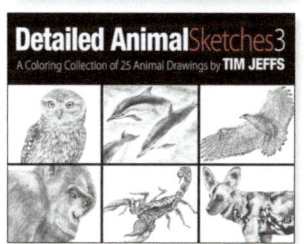 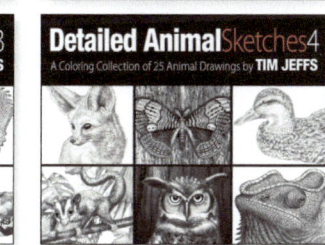 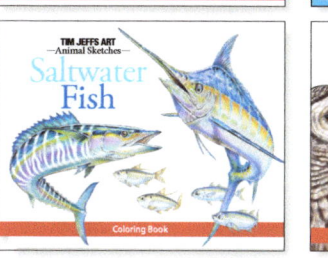 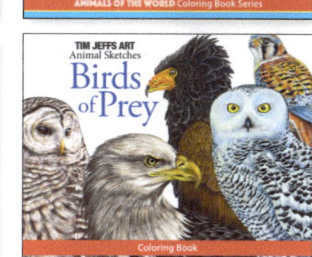
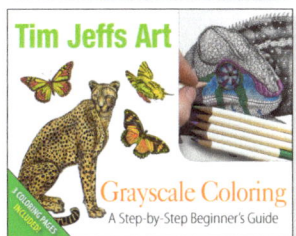 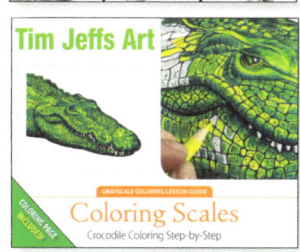 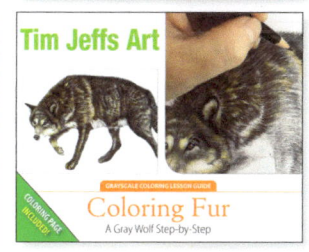 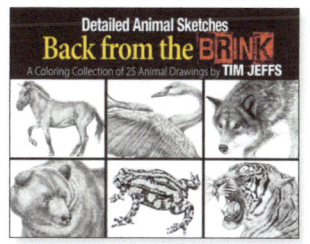 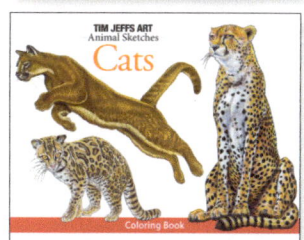
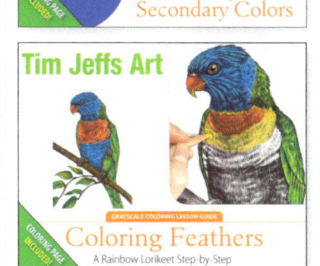 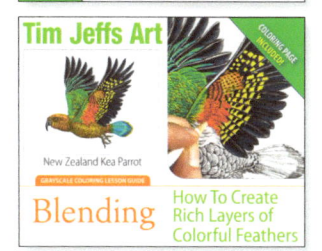 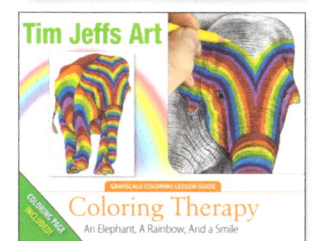 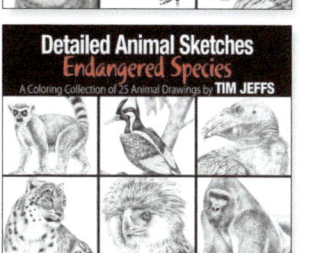 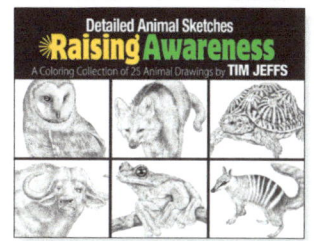

TIM JEFFS ART Online Resources

Share Your Creativity with the World!

Join the ever-expanding coloring group of animal lovers who inspire each other through their colorings of the animals from Tim's books and lessons. With thousands of members from all around the world, Tim's Facebook group "Intricate Ink Coloring Group" is a creative and safe space where everyone is welcome. Jo Warren, the groups all-inspiring administrator will welcome you in with open arms and is there to encourage everyone to just have fun no matter your coloring skill level. Come join, we can't wait to have you as a member! Join Tim's Facebook Coloring Group at:

www.facebook.com/groups/intricateink

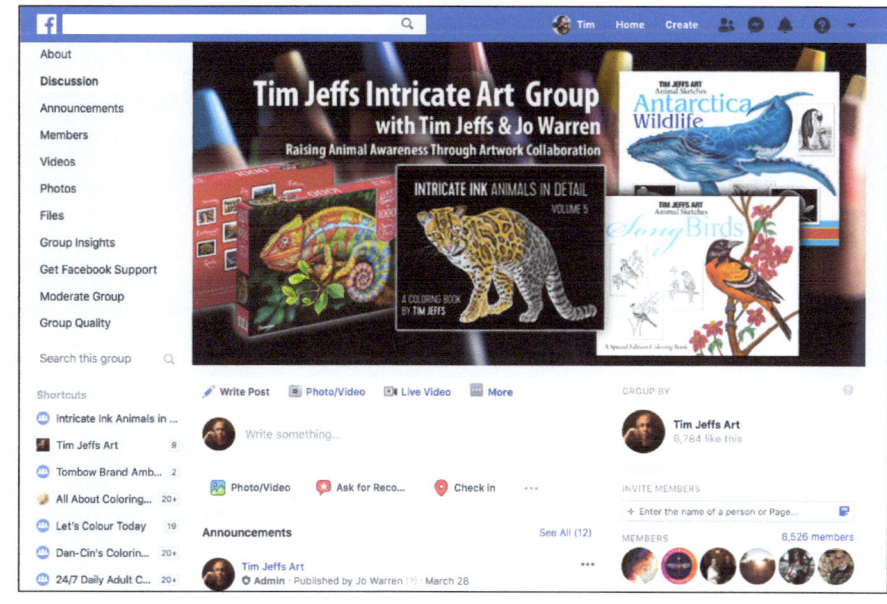

Visit the Home of Tim Jeffs Art

TimJeffsArt.com is my home on the web where I display all of my work and various projects. I hope you can stop by for a visit! You'll find my new shop where signed and unsigned prints of all of my animal drawings are available to purchase, along with the complete library of my digital download coloring books and grayscale coloring lessons. In the conservation section, you can see the projects that I am very proud of. Using my art to preserve wildlife is so important to me.

www.TimJeffsArt.com

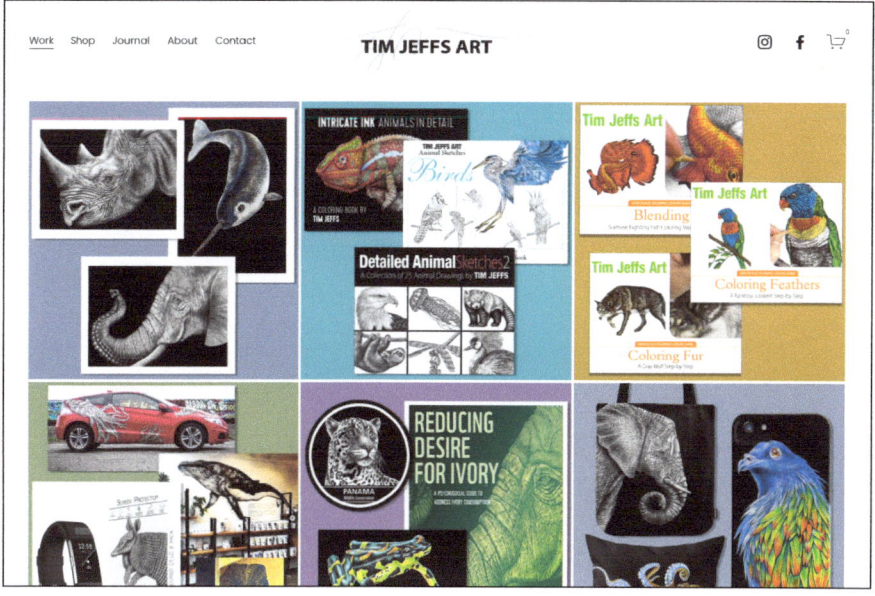